Mother Teresa

Terry Barber

ACTIVIST SERIES

Mother Teresa is published by
Grass Roots Press, a division of Literacy Services of Canada Ltd.

PHONE 1–888–303–3213
WEBSITE www.literacyservices.com

ACKNOWLEDGEMENTS

We would like to thank Linda Schaefer for supplying the majority of the photographs. To view additional images, visit Linda's website at www.motherteresaofcalcutta.com.

We acknowledge the financial support of the Government of Canada through the Book Publishing Industry Development Program (BPIDP) for our publishing activities.

We acknowledge the support of the Alberta Foundation for the Arts for our publishing programs.

Editor: Dr. Pat Campbell
Image Research: Dr. Pat Campbell
Book design: Lara Minja, Lime Design Inc.

Library and Archives Canada Cataloguing in Publication

Barber, Terry, date
    Mother Teresa / written by Terry Barber ; edited by Pat Campbell.

(Activist series)
ISBN 1–894593–48–0

    1. Teresa, Mother, 1910–1997. 2. Missionaries of Charity—Biography.
3. Nuns—India—Calcutta—Biography. 4. Readers for new literates.
I. Campbell, Pat, 1958- II. Title. III. Series.

PE1126.N43B3618 2006   428.6'2   C2006–902735–8

Printed in Canada

Contents

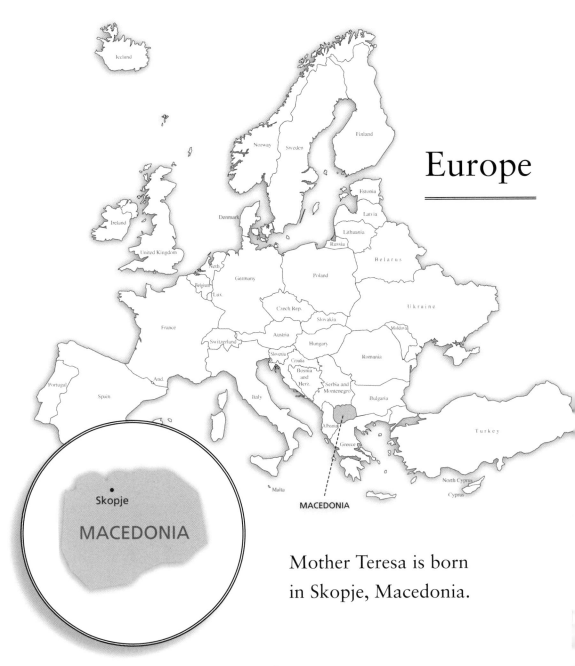

Europe

Skopje

MACEDONIA

MACEDONIA

Mother Teresa is born
in Skopje, Macedonia.

Early Years

 A child is born in Macedonia. She is born in 1910. Her name is Agnes. When she is 12, her life changes. Agnes hears the call of God. Agnes wants to serve God. Agnes wants to serve the poor.

Agnes has an older brother and sister.

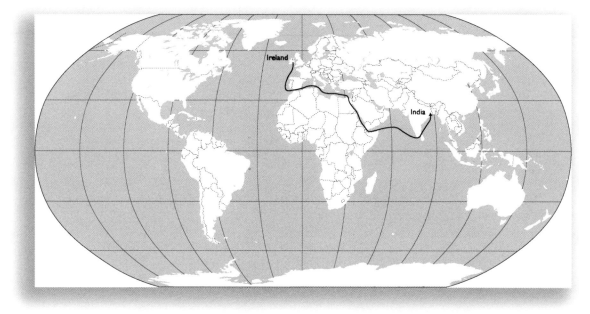

Mother Teresa sails from Ireland to India.

Early Years

Agnes is 18 years old. She wants to be a nun. Agnes moves to Dublin, Ireland. She joins an **order** of Irish nuns. The order sends her to India.

Agnes takes her **vows** as a nun. She will become known as Mother Teresa.

She sails to India on December 1, 1928.

Mother Teresa becomes a nun.

This is one of the **convent** schools in India.

The Slums of Calcutta

Mother Teresa teaches school in Calcutta. The school is for girls. She teaches from 1931 to 1946. She helps many students to learn. She works hard as a teacher. She cares about her students.

Mother Teresa teaches at the Loreto Convent School.

These people live in a tent village.

The Slums of Calcutta

Mother Teresa lives in a **convent.** On Sundays, she visits the poor. She visits hungry people. She visits sick people. She visits dying people. These people are the "poorest of the poor."

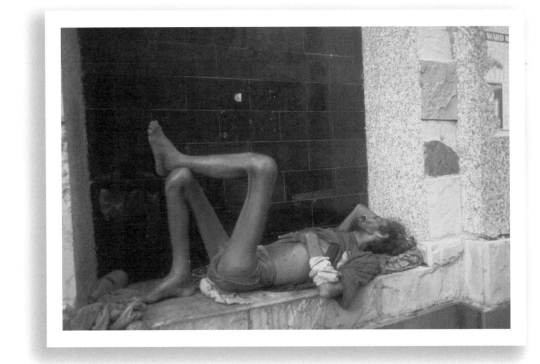

Mother Teresa helps the "poorest of the poor."

The Slums of Calcutta

Mother Teresa sees people who live on the street. They have no place to sleep. They have never slept on a bed. They go to sleep hungry. They sleep on the dirty streets of Calcutta.

Mother Teresa smiles as she works.

Mother Teresa's Work

It is 1946. Mother Teresa hears the call of God again. God tells her to live with the poor. It is the call within the call. In 1948, Mother Teresa leaves the convent. Her life's work is about to begin.

These children go to a school in the slums.

Mother Teresa's Work

Mother Teresa opens a school in the slums. The school has no walls. The school has no books. The school has no blackboards. Mother Teresa uses a stick to write letters in the mud. The poor children learn to read and write.

These people live in the slums of Calcutta.

Mother Teresa's Work

Mother Teresa sees people die on the streets. They need to see doctors. They need medicine. But they have no money. Mother Teresa wants to care for the poor and sick. She wants to learn basic medicine.

This nun treats a woman.

Mother Teresa's Work

Mother Teresa learns basic medicine. She learns how to give needles. She learns how to treat open sores. She learns how to treat diseases. Now she can help sick people.

Mother Teresa learns medicine in Patna, India in 1948.

These women help and love the poor.

Mother Teresa's Work

People hear about Mother Teresa's work. The students she used to teach help her. The students learn how to help the poor. They learn how to talk to the poor.

It is not "how much we give, but how much love we put in the giving."

— *Mother Teresa*

This is a Missionaries of Charity home.

The Missionaries of Charity

In 1950, Mother Teresa starts her own order. It is called the Missionaries of Charity. Mother Teresa says people talk *about* "the poor but very few people talk to the poor." The nuns love and care for the poor.

These nuns take their vows.

The Missionaries of Charity

The nuns take a vow of poverty. This means the nuns live like the poor. The nuns dress like the poor. The nuns eat like the poor. The nuns choose to live this way.

Mother Teresa speaks to an anti-abortion group.

The Missionaries of Charity

Mother Teresa loves children. She wants to save the lives of unborn babies. She speaks against abortion. Mother Teresa says: "If a mother can kill her own child, what is there to stop us from killing ourselves or one another? Nothing."

These lepers sift grain.

The Missionaries of Charity

Mother Teresa has a special place in her heart for **lepers.** She opens many clinics for lepers. The nuns give them food. The nuns give them clothes. The nuns give them medicine. The nuns treat the lepers with **dignity.**

This leper weaves.

Many people are afraid of lepers. Mother Teresa teaches people not to be afraid.

The nuns give this man food and shelter.

The Missionaries of Charity

Mother Teresa and the nuns work with the poorest of the poor. No one else will help these people. The nuns give food to the hungry. They give shelter to the homeless. Mother Teresa says, "the poor must know that we love them."

These children are orphans.

The Order Grows

In 1960, Mother Teresa's order starts to grow. The order opens a home for the dying. The order opens a home for children. The order opens many homes across India. Now the poorest of the poor have a home.

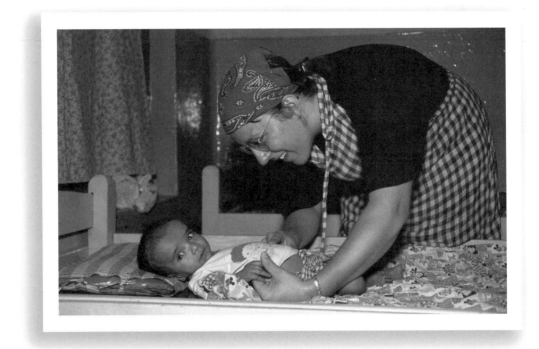

The Order Grows

Today, the Missionaries of Charity has homes in more than 130 countries. There are homes for sick people. The nuns treat about 4 million sick people each year. There are homes for children. The nuns care for 7,000 children each year.

Mother Teresa holds the Nobel Peace Prize.

Mother Teresa Becomes Famous

Mother Teresa wins the Nobel Peace Prize in 1979. People plan a dinner for her. It will cost $7,000. Mother Teresa cancels the dinner. She takes the $7,000. She gives the money to the poor. The money will feed 400 people for a year.

Pope John XXIII gives Mother Teresa a peace prize in 1971.

Mother Teresa lies in an open casket.

Mother Teresa Becomes Famous

Mother Teresa dies on September 5, 1997. She is 87 years old. People from all over the world go to her funeral. The leader of France learns about her death. He says, "there is less love" and "less light in the world."

Mother Teresa lives until she is 87 years old.

Mother Teresa Becomes Famous

Many people think Mother Teresa
is a saint. It takes a long time for the
Catholic Church to give a person this
title. A saint is a special person who
has lived a holy life. Some day Mother
Teresa will be a saint.

Mother Teresa Becomes Famous

Mother Teresa has made the world a better place. She has spread love and peace all over the world. Mother Teresa has helped poor people all over the world. Mother Teresa is gone, but her work lives on.

Glossary

convent: a building where a group
of nuns live.

dignity: the quality of being worthy
of respect.

leper: a person who has leprosy.
Leprosy is a disease.

order: religious people who live under a
common rule. Nuns belong to a religious
order.

vow: a promise.

Talking About the Book

What did you learn about Mother Teresa?

What did you learn about nuns?

Why do you think Mother Teresa left
the convent?

Do you think Mother Teresa is a saint?
Why or why not?

How has Mother Teresa made the world
a better place?

Picture Credits